# Praise for Soundtrack



"Looking back in time through the prism of music, Michael V. Smith crystallizes moments from life, homing in on the safe space music makes for a queer kid, enhancing details or bearing witness to trauma or just letting us live forever even during a plague. This collection is like pulling a well-loved vinyl record from the sleeve and knowing even before you drop the needle you are going deep."
—Brent Bambury, CBC Broadcaster

"Michael V. Smith is at it again. *Soundtrack* gives us an arc we so rarely get, one in which all our preteen longings, our teenage mistakes, our frailties and traumas are just the first verse of a killer song, and it's building to a delirious, cocky, ecstatic final chorus."
—Marcus McCann, author of *Park Cruising*

"*Soundtrack* is a songbook that thrums with heart, hilarity, and moments of brilliance so sharp, wise, and tender I'll carry them with me forever. *Soundtrack* is a testament to the poetics of living and the power of music through Michael V. Smith's essential kaleidoscope of lenses: queer artist, activist, writer, radical, drag diva, humourist, poet, documentarian, and personal DJ."
—Andrea Warner, author of *We Oughta Know: How Céline, Shania, Alanis, and Sarah Ruled the '90s and Changed Music*

Sound
a lyric memoir

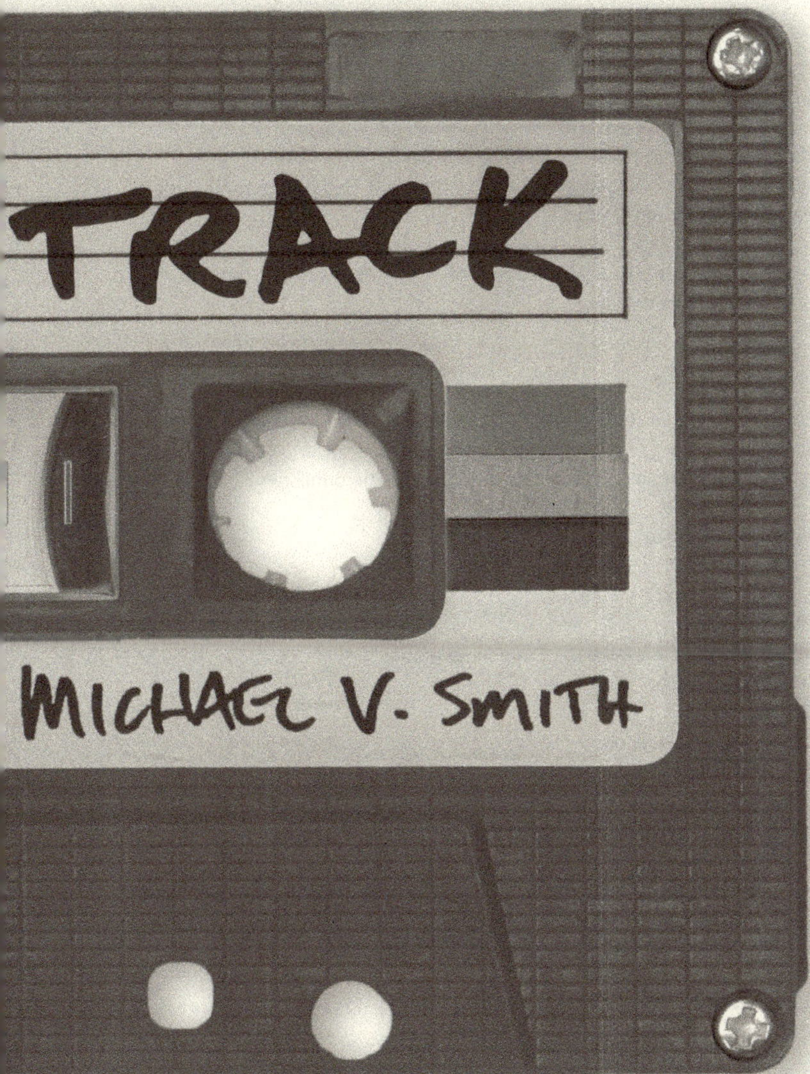


Book*hug Press
Toronto 2025

FIRST EDITION


Library and Archives Canada Cataloguing in Publication

Title: Soundtrack : a lyric memoir / Michael V. Smith.
Names: Smith, Michael V., author
Identifiers: Canadiana (print) 20250205815 | Canadiana (ebook) 20250205823
ISBN 9781771669498 (softcover)
ISBN 9781771669542 (EPUB)
Subjects: LCGFT: Autobiographical poetry. | LCGFT: Poetry.
Classification: LCC PS8587.M5636 S68 2025 | DDC C811/.6—dc23

The production of this book was made possible through the generous assistance of the Canada Council for the Arts and the Ontario Arts Council. Book*hug Press also acknowledges the support of the Government of Canada through the Canada Book Fund and the Government of Ontario through the Ontario Book Publishing Tax Credit and the Ontario Book Fund.

Book*hug Press acknowledges that the land on which we operate is the traditional territory of many nations, including the Mississaugas of the Credit, the Anishnabeg, the Chippewa, the Haudenosaunee, and the Wendat peoples. We recognize the enduring presence of many diverse First Nations, Inuit, and Métis peoples, and are grateful for the opportunity to meet and work on this territory.

Book*hug Press

In loving memory of

Kim Kinakin

March 14, 1971 to September 29, 2024

*We're queer*

*and we're recruiting.*

—The Skinjobs

D90 TRACKS ♡♡♡

A Noise Reduction
EQ Normal : 120μs



B Noise Reduction
EQ Normal : 120μs

Side A

# Parallel Lines

There can only be one Debbie Harry in a white cocktail dress
on the black-and-white striped album cover, standing akimbo

between smiling, shaggy-haired men oblivious to her
best bitch face, fists on her hips. The first I remember

from the handful of records in my parents' collection
that included *Grease* released that same year, Meatloaf's

*Bat Out of Hell*, and Cheech & Chong's *Los Cochinos*.
1978, when I skip through eight tracks to replay songs

so often Mom will yell, *Stop fast-forwarding, you'll wear
the tape out*. When my father and his brothers still comb

their hair straight back like Danny Zuko channelling the king,
Elvis, whose death the previous year made my father sob

at the kitchen table; when Rubik's Cube launches officially
at Studio 54; when Pope John Paul II is inaugurated in

St. Peter's Square while I have lunch with Grandma Cooper
in the Brookdale Mall's Miss Cornwall Restaurant; when

*Dallas*, *Taxi*, *Battlestar Galactica*, *Diff'rent Strokes*, *Mork
& Mindy*, and *WKRP in Cincinnati* all premiere on television.

When the news breaks that Polanski has skipped bail
and America arrests John Wayne Gacy with thirty-three

dead boys in his basement. When my older sister Leica and I
concoct potions with PoP Shoppe cola, lipstick, dead flies,

crayon shavings, and dust bunnies we pinch from under the bed;
when the Montreal Canadiens beat the Bruins to win a third

Stanley Cup in a row, when my father pounds the arm
of his La-Z-Boy hard enough to finally loosen it

into its mythic wobble. When I start bowling five-pin
with my lifetime friend Michael Payne; when Jim Jones

orchestrates a mass suicide and Harvey Milk—whose big gay legacy
I won't know for two more decades—is murdered

in San Francisco City Hall. When HIV is rumoured
to have first penetrated North America. When we are trained

to crouch under our desks at school in nuclear-war drills.
When my neighbour Scott McG and I play a game

of smelling each other's farts. When unbeknownst
to us Blondie plays the El Mocambo in Toronto

on my mother's birthday; when Leica and I dance
in our pajamas in the living room trying not to skip

the needle as we flop our staccato limbs one way
or another, elbows everywhere. When Dad rolls

the car and Mom chains the door to lock him out, again,
Dad begging on the other side of the glass for my sister

or I to unhitch the gold lock and let him in, please
unlock and let him in, please just open the door. When

he punches a hole in a pane and undoes the lock without us,
blood on the window, blood on the floor, blood

on the outside door handle. Before my parents break up
the first time and we sell this house where I learn

a trick to keep myself alive, to not move, to lie perfectly
still, to dissociate, to disappear into every Nancy Drew and

Hardy Boys mystery I can find. When I discover music
drowns the noise too. Music, music in my headphones.

# Thriller

arrives with the body
of my sister's brief
new boyfriend
Jesse
who brings the cassette over
after school—
cassettes being the new
big deal
because
they're way smaller
than eight-tracks,
have songs on *two* sides
and can be rewound.

Leica met Jesse at General Vanier,
grade nine, two years ahead of me.
I've just turned eleven, so Leica
is pushing thirteen.

Jesse probably has the first mullet
I've seen, well before
they'll become a small-town conformity
for hockey jocks.

All those loose curls kissing
the back of his neck.

Though he and my sister don't date
more than a few weeks—I think
they break up over a call
on the rotary phone—
a lot of info about that guy
still rattles around in my head.

Jesse in his denim jacket
with the upturned collar
at our particleboard
kitchen table. My parents
out for the night.
                    Jesse burns
a small blob of thick shiny black paste
between two knives he's heated up
on the red coils of the stove.

*What's that*, I ask, and he,
with the shell of a BIC pen
between his lips
says, *Motorcycle grease*.

His wisp of a moustache,
pierced left earlobe

—when the right ear
signals gay, though lots of folks
in '83 think any man
with an earring
is a fag.

Jesse sports a dangly
sterling pair of handcuffs
because, my sister explains,
Jesse has moved from Toronto
where all the big city kids
wear an earring.

Not a week or so into school
some thug rips the mini-handcuffs
clear through his earlobe—
conformity violence
a strategy
small-town men use
as social control.

I'll be too afraid
to get my own
George Michael hoops
until thirty-one.

Nobody has seen anything
like *Thriller*'s music
video, its large ensemble
dance numbers, zombies
of small-town men
and women.

How MJ
rebrands as a solo artist
moonwalking
into culture
a.k.a. white culture
a.k.a. prime time TV

a red leather jacket
white socks
under tight black pants
short at the ankle

one white glove.

Metonymies
to outlast the hard news stories
that will follow
about boys my age.

I learn to dance watching videos
from that album. I thrust
my knees forward and flip
onto the tips of my shoes

in a signature
Billie Jean ballerina
redux, balancing
on a dance floor

at the edge of my body
like I might hold
the world at bay

with the same exquisite tenderness
I imagine Jesse holds
in his denim-clad arms.

# Colour by Numbers

For a brief moment in the early '80s, Darrin waltzes into grade five as the cute new boy all the girls giggle over, until some other transfer kid from their previous school reveals Darrin's old trick of twirling like Wonder Woman, that he happily demonstrates.

Popularity is a light switch.

The upper-level boys know enough about desire and the school ground to turn Kristy's crush on Darrin into an excuse to pin his gangly arms and legs in the grass at lunchtime so she can brand him with a massive hickey.

Juvenile normcore training, or, how to get in with the boys.

I watch his exasperated sobbing and say nothing, rationalizing my passivity makes me as close to an ally as possible, without becoming a target myself.

For my fiftieth birthday, Darrin will surprise me with a letter:

*You made it this far*
*and I'm pretty sure there were times*
*you didn't think you would;*

*I know that feeling so well.*

By grade seven he and I hang out enough to get into the trouble of innocents: he pierces his own ear in front of me with a boiled needle and ice cube, we string reems of audiotape from a broken cassette between hydro poles across Third Street, at dusk, then from his second-storey window we wait for a car, until we spy a cyclist and have to scream, *Stop stop!*

We howl at everything, eager to be loose with the world.

*I can't for the life of me find it*<br>
*but there is a picture*<br>
*out there somewhere*<br>
*of you and I together*<br>
*at one of my birthday parties*<br>
*(12 or 13 yrs old)*<br>
*and I'm holding up a card*<br>
*and a five-dollar bill*<br>
*you gave me.*

We take to wandering our paper-mill town with Michael Payne, living our best music-video fantasy. Michael and I compete to wear a plastic Viking helmet with horns, a favourite prop.

Darrin's homemade braids, a kaftan from his mother, Cleopatra eyeliner, and ropes of beads make him a terrific Boy George look-alike.

Many straight viewers watching "Karma Chameleon" the first time replay the tired old trope of wondering aloud if Boy George *is* in fact a boy. While the rest of us see ourselves on TV for the first time. That aha moment. A culture club.

*I can still feel the excitement*
*written on my face as it was*
*the first time I'd felt*
*as though someone*
*in this world*
*understood me.*

I don't know who has the idea, but Darrin, me, and two guys from our elementary class register in an air-band competition in grade seven. Darrin lights across the stage in his white kaftan and faux braids convincingly enough to win us a spot competing city-wide at the Civic Complex a month later, but in the end our skinny limbs and blue jeans are no competition for Twisted Sister.

*You did absolutely nothing, just*
*the fact of you being there,*
*your energy.*

When I walk into Darrin's room one afternoon to find him sitting on the edge of his bed naked, counting his pubes (three!) that's too much for me. Too intimate. Too gay. Too much skin. I never hang out with Darrin again.

Let me scratch out the hold-his-head-in-a-flushing-toilet bullying I witness Darrin survive in high school. Nobody wants to remember what that was like, right?

*You were emanating something*
*I identified with, don't know*
*how else to explain it.*

*I knew then I wasn't alone, and*
*I thank you for this gift,*
*more so than the five bucks.*

I'm amazed at Darrin, again, sending me a letter like this, because I know myself as that kid who steps back, deliberately, who chooses to hide in the shadows, with thanks in no small part to Darrin's light.

# She's So Unusual

In November of grade eight, the older
siblings of D and Matthew
arrange for all of us
to see Cyndi Lauper
at the Ottawa Ex, in the same arena
I'd watch the Cornwall Royals
play Junior A hockey.
                                        Maybe
it's the familiarity of the venue
but I'm surprised I've managed
to convince my parents
to let me travel an hour away
with teenagers.

I'm thirteen. I've never
been out of town without a parent.

Our group joins another.
We rendezvous
with the siblings' friends
in a farmhouse in Apple Hill
as rural as it sounds.

                                        That host
also brings a younger brother,
my age, with smooth skin, dark eyes
and a spiky blond haircut
full of goop.

We all sit around the table
in the wallpapered kitchen, gabbing.
I've never hung out with older teens
like this, no adults.
I can barely follow
the jokes, but I laugh along regardless.

I've been training for years
to make myself small, to vanish
in front of people.

The boy in the farmhouse
sits at the head of the table.

His sister applies a long piece
of Scotch tape below
both of his Dutch cheekbones

then

uses a light finger under his chin
to move his head from side to side
applying a hot pink blush
thick
across his cheeks.

When she removes the tape
a creamy strip of bare skin
streaks up the middle
of all that pink

I can almost imagine
a runway
for my tongue.

Done, she turns to us and asks
if anyone else
wants some.
                    Terrified
to speak, I try to make
my body as indistinct
as possible.

I don't know anyone in Cornwall
who doesn't wear blue jeans
or track pants every day. Nobody
will sport Manic Panic hair colours
for another three years, save Darrin
who'll come to grade-eight graduation
with red food colouring in his hair
spiked by sugar water
that will melt in the heat
of the outdoor ceremony
down the side of his face.

To answer the sister
with a blush brush in hand
someone at the kitchen table lobs
a joke:
            *Not gonna happen.*

I miss my moment.

We pile in the back
of a white rental van
and ride to Ottawa seatless

which feels illicit
cuz my parents
would never have allowed us
to ride without a seat belt.

In the Civic Centre
not twenty feet from the stage
we stand on the floor
usually covered in ice
where I've seen
the Ottawa Senators skate.

The Bangles open Cyndi's show
though this tour must have helped
make them. None of us will know
who they are until later that fall
when their video with Leonard Nimoy
appears on *Video Hits*.
                                        Cyndi
emerges in a giant sun hat and signature
layers of skirts and beads
everyone at the time says Madonna
copied from her.

Orange hair
fading to yellow at the tips, buzzed
at the sides
Cyndi is a marvel.

That crystalline voice, needle
sharp on the fast songs, then pillow soft
for "Time After Time."
Cyndi, our future
queer hero, she-bops
on speakers right
above me and my friends
too terrified to dance.

I can't believe that's *her*.

I want Cyndi's sweat
to bless my forehead

anoint the tongue
of my open mouth
turn me
into someone more
than this self-conscious
shuffler I'm dying
to undo.

# Purple Rain

Queerly beloved,
I watch *Purple Rain*
at the Brookdale Cinemas
before I ever hear the album. I think
I go with Todd T, whose mother
adores me. I'm always more popular
with people's parents
or pets
          though Todd,
for some reason, takes to me one summer.

For years every time
I mention his name
my mom will ask, *Is that*
*the kid from your birthday party*
*who threw up at Pondarosa*?

                    *Yes, Mom. That's*
*the same Todd.*

He and I see movies together.
*Gremlins* and *Ghostbusters* screen
that same year. I can't wait to spend
my paper route money sitting in the dark
theatre with Todd, my secret hero.

After he'd caught Eric Laframboise
bullying me, Todd began
a pushing match, threatening
to fight Eric if he ever
picked on me again.

Todd and I weren't friends
yet. I don't know why
Todd swept in
to protect me.

Nobody but my sister
looks out for me
and she's graded out
to a different school

so I'm warm-in-the-belly
enamoured by this
popular boy
who's standing up for me.

In the preteen '80s
pre-internet, I know nothing
about how boys tick
except for what I'm not
supposed to do.

Nobody
succeeds at failing
quite like me.

One evening in the back
parking lot of that same cinema
Michael Payne and I exit
*The Goonies* when a friendly
red-headed man in his thirties
asks us what we thought
of the movie, then offers us
a ride home
cuz it's late.

We decline.

Moments later
he pulls up beside us in his car
with the window down
to double-check
if we're okay.

*Why don't you boys just get in*
*and talk, I want to ask you*
*something, here*
he leans over
opens the door
*hop in, just for a minute.*

We have a long exchange
wherein he offers
a variety of options
for who to drop off first
till we're a definitive
*No*,
and start to walk away.

His car creeps
through the parking lot
waiting to see
in which direction we'll head
but we lose him by doubling back
through a graveyard.

This is before
cameras
line the streets

when it's easier
to make a boy
disappear.

*Purple Rain*
the first of Prince's albums
on the Billboard 200
to reach number one

twenty-five million copies sold

one of the bestselling albums
of all time, wins the Oscar
for best original score

but I don't remember much
about what Todd and I think
of the movie. Or Prince.
His tight pants. His preteen
moustache, sure.
Maybe the movie blurs
with my preoccupation
with the boy sitting beside me.

Todd

lives in a wartime house
much like my own, two bedrooms
on the narrow second floor, one
for his parents and one he shares
with his older brother. Their beds
tucked on either side of the room
beneath a sloped ceiling.

At a dizzying sleepover,
Todd insists I take his bed
while he lounges
on an air mattress
beside me.

Around nine, he draws a bath
in the washroom at the top of the stairs
between bedrooms.

Todd's mill-working, thick-
in-the-shoulders father
hasn't finished renovating
the bathroom

bearing only
a makeshift curtain

so each time Todd moves
I can hear his gestures
in a gurgle of water.

That
pearl
strings together
with a dewdrop from humping
the swing set a little extra
when I climb its poles

and a gossamer dream
of my father walking in on me
sexing an alien

with a long narrow shaft

like a stamen
from their belly button
before I know a thing
about penetration.

Correct: my first
nocturnal emission
features an alien.
[takes a bow]

1984.

A nod
to the dystopian novel, sure,
the year HIV spreads
across the news
as the cause of AIDS

while Todd's boy body
places a finger
on a trigger in mine.

Sleeping giants.

Todd and I stop hanging soon after
he loses his virginity
with my then
best friend Becky
in the summer between
grades eight and nine.

I go to a different high school
so I don't see Todd again
even in our small town
until probably
a decade later at a wedding.

By then, I've come out.

At the reception, Todd pretends
he doesn't see me.

I almost
don't blame him.
Boys learn caution
like we learn sex:
word of mouth
or experience, a swish
of water behind
a bathroom curtain.

Boys being boyish, we're less
concerned with the truth
of who we are
than who might threaten
our image.

Todd
and I know nothing
about queerness
except rumour,
name-calling, AIDS
on the news, everyone
with an opinion to share

about the fictions
we don't yet know
we aren't.

# No Borders Here

My first visit to D's house
        thirteen
        a full decade before
        she will come out as trans, both of us
        pretending to be boys
        everyone wants us to be
D pulls out this record
from a stack, saying,
                *You* have
                *to hear this.*

Everything about this visit
intimidates me. D's family has a bedroom
nobody sleeps in — reserved for guests.
A tan leather couch they call
a loveseat. A shiny black piano.
In the basement, a drum kit,
a photographer's darkroom,
and in the far corner
an area on the floor covered
with a massive piece of cardboard
for breakdancing — D tries
to teach me some moves.

Even the album itself
gobsmacks me:

I've never bought a record.
D has enough money
to buy her own album.
A stack of them.

It hasn't occurred to me
you could buy your own music.
My naive blue-collar ass learning
how other people live. *Rich people*,
I would say, not knowing
anything about the upper
middle class.

Sitting on that leather loveseat
hanging out with a doctor's kid
I feel my life expanding.

In four years
D and I will be seventeen
still listening to Siberry

slowly confessing
our mutual love, in veiled language

> *I think I feel*
> *a kind of love*
> *for you...like*
> *Darrin.*

> *Oh yeah, I think*
> *I do too.*

at the same time
D starts dating
one of my best
women friends.

On our days off, D and I talk music.
Hours of leaning into each other
interpreting
Siberry's songs

"Dancing Class" replays
a lesbian love affair, right?
She must be queer—look at that
asymmetrical haircut.

"Mimi on the Beach" the best
fuck-the-normcore anthem.

So much so we develop
an elaborate code

a twin language

but the gay kind

subtext

    hankie code
    harmonies

based on songs
and private conversations.

We source lyrics
for communicating
our feelings
about this joy
or that devastation.

When friends are around

we speak one language
with a small comment
on a lyric,

and counterpoint
an undertone

"I love you"
or
"I'm feeling super
fucking jealous
of my other
best friend
sitting next to you
up front
in the station wagon
holding your hand"
or
"Let's try penetration
again tonight."

Teenage stuff.

I'm a seventeen-year-old
suicidal fag in a mill-working family,
the sissy who can never do anything
right
          in love for the first time
with my best friend

who swaps blow jobs with me
for three hours
every night
but who is dating me
in secret
while also dating
my other
best friend.

               Siberry's
               "You Don't Need"
is a shorthand:

*I think it is the hardest*
*when I see you look at her*
*in a way I thought was*
*ooooonly meant for meee,*
*inspired by me.*

I make a lot of compromises
to be in love that first time.

No doubt, D does too.

I spend a lot of lunch hours
exhausted, trying
to find places to hide
from my friends

[besides the drama room
where we all hide
from the rest of the school]

to cry and gnash my teeth
and try to get my shit together
so nobody can tell
I'm tormented
inside of a love
I have to share

in some cheesy
bi-teen love triangle
Afterschool Special.

But
        I want to linger
in the thrill of D
in the piano room
this first time

holding out
in the space
between our bodies

*No Borders Here*

what I don't yet know
will be the soundtrack
to my first queer kiss

on the lips
of this young person
right here, grinning with the joy
of introducing me
to something new.

# Love's Gonna Get Ya

A crooner for Patches, our calico
who loves me through childhood.

Calicoes are female, I tell everyone
who hasn't asked and likely

already knows. Rusty
all over, even her white

looks peppered with dirt
that we claim was stained

from a bucket of oil
she fell in as a kitten.

We spend years
mistakenly claiming this.

When my parents finally split
I move out of the house

with my mother,
which feels impossible

despite knowing we'll survive it,
so we leave my father

the cat. *We can't take Patches*
*away from him too,*

we debate aloud to hear if the tenor
of the words holds true.

When I come for visits, Dad plays
"Love's Gonna Get Ya!"

on repeat, while sobbing
at the kitchen table.

I've hated Ricky Skaggs
for a long time, but now

the timbre of his voice is more
a welcome reminder

for how death changes
our relationship to things.

Patches, my great love,
responds to our departure

by defecating
pretty much anywhere

in the finished basement.
She wanders

the house meowling. *Why*
*have you left me?*

*Here's what I think*
*of your empty rooms.*

# The Lion + the Cobra

I remember it, six weeks
of summer

with Sinéad O'Connor

a new voice
of god, raging
in my headphones

prostrate
on my sister's couch

after my mother kicks me
out of the house

at sixteen.

We've fought
about the smallest thing

that ballooned
until I dissociate
and notice I'm yelling
so hard

spit drools
down my face.

*Woah,*
*that's weird*

I say, inside,
while the outer me

keeps hollering.

This is my body.

My body is this
creature with a second
mind
          beyond
          my conscious control

like erections,
am I right, guys?

A humiliating Whac-A-Mole
in my pants

every day

the love-shame vice
of navigating
high school hallways
with a no-good-reason
boner in my pants

carrying a stack of books
to hide the bulge
as some guy
whispers
over my shoulder
*sotto voce* *Hey, Faggot*

in my ear, his breath
viral

spearmint
aftershave

At night, I perform
a series of push-ups
or use the bunk bed
above me to bench press
its weight

*Faggot, hey,*
*how many dicks*
*did you suck off*
*last night,*
*Faggot?*

but my stick arms refuse
to grow anything
but hair.

The antidote:
teaching myself where to focus
so my eyes never
make contact
with a boy

act

normal, erase myself
learn too well
how people work.

My classic erasure
in the hallways

*Ya, Faggot,*
*how many?*

convinces people
to like me
by swallowing

*Why won't you*
*answer me,*
*Faggot?*

the queer self

a survival instinct
most faggots learn
alone.

I can't explain
how devastating it is
to know so many
young queers today

likely know this too                                        *Yeah, you.*
regardless
of the year they were born.
                                                    Time
after time, we eat ourselves
to prevent being
eaten.

When my mother and I are done
I storm to my room
for no more than a minute
of silence, before the door
opens to three
black garbage bags
and my mother saying
flatly

*Hey Faggot, what's*
*in yer mouth?*

*Pack your things.*
*I called your father.*
*He's coming to get you.*

This is during one
of those times when
my sister has let Dad
move into their spare room
of their two-bedroom
apartment, rather than risk
him being homeless.

*What's in yer mouth?*

Just before Leica
and Rolland are accepted
into social housing

where they'll be able
to afford kids.

Leica at eighteen, with her father
the dependent.
There's a reason
she's so good
at raising children.

My father and I
will live together
for six weeks.

*Why won't you*
*answer me?*

One last time.

*Faggot?*

When I'm not sleeping
on the couch in the living room
I'm listening to Sinéad
belt out
my emotional tenor.

*Stupid, Faggot.*

One night, someone
at the dinner table jokes
that we make an elite club:

Mom has now
kicked each of us
out of the house
at least once.

I'm struggling
how to hold this
without causing more harm
to a mother
who barely had
her own childhood.

I don't want to overlook
the ways my mother was capable
of mothering.

*I see you. Hey.*

As she unboxes more
of her story, beyond
the expected stresses
when teenagers
have children

the years
remake themselves.

Much like Sinéad's
shaved head

is a lesson
in reframing
not skinhead

*Did you miss me,*
*Faggot?*

but a counter-tenor
to norms
that would reduce her
to skinhead.

*Yeah, that's*
*what I thought.*

Like
how taking adoptive
parenting classes
has taught me to hear

beyond my mother's
own adoption

a distortion.

Comparison, then,
becomes a spotlight
I shine on the past
gently, in much
the same way a poem
about a woman
whose voice
could cut glass

alive
when I began writing

rings
differently
before I can finish.

*C'mere, Faggot*

*I got something*
*for you.*

My mother
allows me to return home
six weeks later
after I handwrite a letter
that dodges
through coded language
that I'm gay, but confessed
I've been suicidal
for years.

*That's right, Faggot.*

*You better run.*

# We Are the Champions

It's 1986. People are dying faster
than newspapers can print.
Queen stops performing
live with Freddie Mercury

diagnosed
HIV positive
in secret
the following year.

To protect his family
from the inevitable
media harassment

Freddie refuses to reveal his status
until '91, the day before
he dies.

His cause of death prompts journalists
to write columns in national papers
declaring they would shoot
their own sons
if they had AIDS

which isn't news to queers
who know how much
better off we are
dead
than in families
like those.

You can understand
why Freddie might have wanted
to spare his family
the ugly truth
of what people
can become.

On those days
my parents are growing
apart, I escape to Reneal Street

to Michael Payne's home
where I can feel joy
without fear
for what might come next.

Every time I return home
I walk into our house
not knowing what might
have happened
in my absence. Each return
requires emotional resolve.

I visit Reneal for so long
so often, I begin to call
Michael Payne's mother
*Mom*.

Claire told me this past year
had she known how bad it was
at home, she'd have offered
to let me move in with them
though neither of us
could have imagined a world
where that would have been possible.

My first time visiting, Mom
sits on the floral-print couch
plucking the hairs from her legs
with tweezers. *If you destroy the root*,
she explains, *eventually*
*you won't have to shave*.

By contrast, Kenny Payne
shaves his thick stubble
every morning before work
and again
when he arrives home.

I think Michael Payne's family rich
for having an above-ground pool
ten feet in diameter.

Every sunny day, Kenny
will lie out on the deck
alone, the blinds drawn
—you can't disturb him—
to expose his psoriasis to the sun.

Kenny prayed through his twenties,
Mom tells me, until the day
a doctor diagnosed
Michael's scaly spot
and Kenny stopped believing.

No god
could wish this on his son.

Everyone's kind of handsome
Kenny sports a big smile, grey eyes,
I think.
            It's been so long
I remember only the pitter-pat
warmth when he laughs
at something I've said
before I know what it is
to love a man
I wish could be
my father.

The Paynes take me
with them on weekends
to softball tournaments

where Michael and I
watch the game
or troll through the bush
till we collapse
in our pup tent.

One afternoon
I come by after school
while Michael's parents
scream at each other.

He and I make ourselves scarce
in the backyard eating
Dairy Queen cones trying not
to overhear.

This
rarely happens; these two
don't fight.

A week later, Kenny moves in
with a girlfriend he met golfing,
buys a white Corvette
I spy everywhere
even years afterward
though I barely ever
see him again.

Michael will update me
some days
                    as I secretly
wish I can ask for my own
parental visits.

Kenny becomes
a story we share.

Something mythic
like the chemo

waltzing through Kenny's body
until moving a sofa bed
he collapses
of a heart attack.

At the funeral, his best friend
I know from their softball tourneys
cries so hard
he can't finish
the eulogy.
                    The first time
I see a man
other than my father
weep.

Over the years Michael Payne
will comment, *You cried more*
*at my father's funeral*
*than I did.*
Guilty
of doing the same
at his mother's service.

Claire passed this summer

a week after I texted
an image of the inscription
in my first writing journal
that she'd bought for me.

> *I believe that putting down on paper*
> *a thought, sorrow or joy*
> *relieves your mind and heart*
> *as it embeds a memory.*

*Love, Mom*
*Claire Payne*

When my own father died
I grieved both the man I'd lost
and a father I never really had.

For Claire, I'm grieving
a mother I did have.

At the end of Kenny's service
they play "We Are the Champions"
which still ruins me
every time.

After Kenny's funeral, a dozen
of Michael's friends
all dressed up
go for drinks
at Freddy's Tavern.

We're laughing till we cry
with that joy
death reminds us to gather
everywhere possible.

The waitress asks us,
*What's the occasion?*

It takes some awkward patience
to convince her
Kenny Payne is dead.

# Kiss Me, Kiss Me, Kiss Me

I'm recording a cover version
of this first love, but bringing in
The Cure.

My high-school bestie Mimi
swoons over Robert Smith
on the Kiss Tour in 1987
about two weeks before
Michael Payne plays me
The Cure
for the first time.

*Japanese Whispers*.
"The Walk."

When she waltzes into Drama Club
in a concert T-shirt in September
I give her a hard time
for not telling me
about the show.

> *I did tell you*, Mimi counters.
> *You didn't know who they were.*

And I answer something like
*But you didn't tell me hard enough*.

One morning in grade eleven, Mimi
comes to school with her hair spiked
like Howard Jones: shaved sides,
frosted tips. I'm pining
to do a copy but can't
figure out how you just change
[*snaps fingers*]
overnight.

Some mornings I take an hour
to dress. I walk the line
trying to live my flashy
new wave dream

but still be boring
enough
to never stand out.
                                        Cornwall clothing
can make the difference
between life
or death.
                    Like Mimi's gay hairdresser
                    who gets jumped
                    by a group of men
                    in a crowded bar.

They send him
to the Hotel Dieu Hospital
in a coma.

Everyone in town hears
though I don't believe the local paper
runs a story.

That same summer
Liberace's face is plastered
across tabloids, not finally
a story about his closeted life
but his sensational demise:

complications from AIDS

selling even more papers.

Two months later, Princess Di
shakes hands with an AIDS patient, the photo
a gunshot heard around the world.

Imagine making international news
because you touch a person
without gloves.
                    Six weeks later
Ronald Reagan
delivers his first speech
about AIDS.

I feel so cool
when I buy *Kiss Me,
Kiss Me, Kiss Me*

with my gas-station-attendant
paycheque

and hyperaware
of being hot hot hot
for some gorgeous someone

                    my eye
on D, who's irresistible

kissable.

I'm smitten and bitten
and hooked and cooked

and stuck like glue.

I'm ready to be a practising
homosexual, any day now,
thank you.

This is about the time Cleve Jones creates the AIDS quilt, a public memorial to protest our recent dead. 1,300,000 square feet of panels handmade 3×6, to echo a coffin's dimensions.

Throughout these years
Grandma Cooper
often mentions

Lorne Littlejohn

                    a family friend.

Blond
a favourite
of my grandmother

Lorne moved to Toronto
cuz he likes to wear dresses.

I never meet him except
through family lore.

The first
out gay man
my family knows

dies in 1988.

I've seen his fabric plot
on the AIDS quilt.

Every homo alive
during this time
has a story
about their first fag
who died.

I allow myself
sexual attraction
when being light
in the loafers
is considered prancing
toward an early death.

A community
of gay men

steps ahead of me
becoming

endless

static

their chorus of silence

silence silence silence silence silence silence silence silence silence
silence silence silence silence silence silence silence silence silence
silence silence silence silence silence silence silence silence silence
silence silence silence silence silence silence silence silence silence
silence silence silence silence silence silence silence silence silence
silence silence silence silence silence silence silence silence silence
silence silence silence silence silence silence silence silence silence
silence silence silence silence silence silence silence silence silence
silence silence silence silence silence silence silence silence silence
silence silence silence silence silence silence silence silence silence
silence silence silence silence silence silence silence silence silence
silence silence silence silence silence silence silence silence silence
silence silence silence silence silence silence silence silence silence
silence silence silence silence silence silence silence silence silence
silence silence silence silence silence silence silence silence silence
silence silence silence silence silence silence silence silence silence
silence silence silence silence silence silence silence silence silence
silence silence silence silence silence silence silence silence silence
silence silence silence silence silence silence silence silence silence
silence silence silence silence silence silence silence silence silence
silence silence silence silence silence silence silence silence silence
silence silence silence silence silence silence silence silence silence
silence silence silence silence silence silence silence silence silence
silence silence silence silence silence silence silence silence silence
silence silence silence silence silence silence silence silence silence
silence                         silence silence silence silence silence
silence silence silence silence silence silence silence silence silence
silence silence silence silence silence silence silence silence silence
silence silence silence silence silence silence silence silence silence
silence silence silence silence silence silence silence silence silence

silence silence silence silence silence silence silence silence silence
silence silence silence silence silence silence silence silence silence
silence silence silence silence silence silence silence silence silence
silence silence silence silence silence silence silence silence silence
silence silence silence silence silence silence silence silence silence
silence silence silence silence silence silence silence silence silence
silence silence silence silence silence silence silence silence silence
silence silence silence silence silence silence silence silence silence
silence silence silence silence silence silence silence silence silence
silence silence silence silence silence silence silence silence silence
silence silence silence silence silence silence silence silence silence
silence silence silence silence silence silence silence silence silence
silence silence silence silence silence silence silence silence silence
silence silence silence silence silence silence silence silence silence
silence silence silence silence silence silence silence silence silence
silence silence silence silence silence silence silence silence silence
silence silence silence silence silence silence silence silence silence
silence silence silence silence silence silence silence silence silence
silence silence silence silence silence silence silence silence silence
silence silence silence silence silence silence silence silence silence
silence silence silence silence silence silence silence silence silence
silence silence silence silence silence silence silence silence silence
silence silence silence silence silence silence silence silence silence
silence silence silence silence silence silence silence silence silence
silence silence silence silence silence silence silence silence silence
silence silence silence silence silence silence silence silence silence
silence silence silence silence silence silence silence silence silence
silence silence silence silence silence silence silence silence silence
silence silence silence silence silence silence silence silence silence
silence silence silence silence silence silence silence silence

= death

The spring of grade twelve
I fall in love, or try to
figure out what love is.

D and I gesture toward sex
with my fingers
touching D's body

    light
    slow
    consistent
    touch
    on either side
    of the bridge
    on D's nose
    in the bowl
    where the tear duct
    rests

via a pretense
of healing with touch
a headache, a stiff
shoulder.

Just after
her messy breakup
with the lead singer
in their band
                    who is twenty-one
                    with a kid.
D and I are seventeen.

Dropping me off at home one night,
D asks whether
she should be dating
anyone new

and I
in my magnanimity

suggest she wait.

She's only just come out
of a tricky relationship

—bandmates, right?—

I don't want to be
just a rebound.

Except

D isn't talking
about me.

D means Mimi.
They've already made out.

Fuck high school.

A month later, D takes Mimi to prom

despite D and I fooling around
in secret
every night

either in D's
faux-wood-panelling station wagon
or her mother's Malibu
with velour seats.

Prom sucks
in the worst way.

I even have to talk my date
into going.
                    I buy a pocket square
to match the peach dress Kathy
finds in Ottawa
                        identical
in every way to the prom dress
on the other Cathy
in our class.

Years later Kathy will tell me
she was convinced
that night
I would try to steal
her virginity.

About this same time
in my final year of high school
I serve on a committee
for teen sexual health awareness

thanks to my English teacher
Ms. MacDonald
who understands AIDS
as a real threat to teens
likely doing more
than their parents
fear.

The forum's keynote speaker
all the way from Ottawa
is a gay lawyer

named Michael Smith.

To protect me, Elaine suggests
they change his name
to Robert Smith.

Irony, you are
filthy
and delicious.

This other Michael Smith
pretending to be Robert

        the first out gay man
        I'm to meet
        in person

arrives at my high school
wearing my exact

same

eyeglasses.

At the keynote address
where AIDS patients
deliver a pointed summary
of their story

D faints
for the first time
ever.

In case you're wondering
what it's like
to be a young queer
staring down the barrel
of your future.

Over drinks to celebrate
the successful end
of that evening, I'm sweating
to come out
to these premier homos

right there, at the same
table with me

but I chicken out
and leave
with Michael Payne

who then forces me
to waltz back in
and tell the other
Michael Smith
I'm gay too.

My beloved doppelganger
just smiles, sweetly,
and says, *Of course you are*
as his buddies
giggle behind their hands.

A month later, spurred
by my well-placed ultimatum
*ahem*
D and Mimi break up.

In my yearbook
a coded entry
for Favourite Moment
reads:

*The Cure and Summer Love*.

At the outdoor bandstand
in Lansdowne Park
during
The Cure's trippy visuals
on their Disintegration Tour

D
holds my hand

beneath the coats
we've placed between us.

    I'm so happy
    I can imagine
    a future.

# Side B

# Enjoy the Silence

Though I've never owned
any Depeche Mode
I might get right
eighty per cent of the words
to this song despite being terrible
at divining lyrics.

Matthew
plays his cassettes
on repeat as he drives us
up and down the streets
of Cornwall on these nights
we have nowhere else
to belong.

Matthew, frizzy
blond hair in a big swoop
side part, dimples, freckles,
and a little round pumpkin nose

Matthew
who was known
in junior high to press
too close to girls
at the school dances
likely more from ignorance
than creep factor
though I suspect
it felt the same
from the girls'
perspective.

At twelve, none of us knew
how to say stop
peddling your erection
on the gymnasium
dance floor.

Now sixteen, with the new
N on his bumper,
Matthew drives the family's
second car, a white boat
I call the DMC
—which bugs him every time—
after I find out the car was bought
from the widow
of his father's friend.
*The Dead Man's Car.*

In and out of town, Matthew and I
will disagree on nearly every
issue we discuss. Debating him
feels like listening to a recap
of whatever article
he's read somewhere.
I tell D
Matthew never has opinions
of his own.
But those nights
he enjoys arguing
and trading ideas
make me
articulate a position

like headlights
for the future.

When D and I come out to him,
Matthew takes it worse
than all my friends
despite coming out himself
two years later.

I can understand
his defensive strategy

yet
D and I are also the last
in our friend group to know.

A year
of whispering.

It's not like we don't
have clues. Depeche Mode?
Words are barely
necessary

but still I'm puzzled why
we were his first friends out
and the last ones told.

That hurts, I guess.

After D and I move
to Toronto for university
Matthew informs us officially
through an invite to Colby's
for a drag show featuring
one of the big queens
Diana Rose maybe
in a small sequin corset
and tight tuck, flirting
with a fan
of ostrich feathers.

Matthew, who has never
seen a queen before,
keeps shouting

*I can't believe*
*that's a man.*
*Where's his penis?*

from the front row

and we're too naive
and shamefaced to do anything
but shush this man
who has kept silent
until now.

# Groove Is in the Heart

By the time I come out
to my stepfather's stepbrother
    Rob, a year older
    from Niagara Falls,
D and I have been blowing
each other for two years
in the family car.

On nights we have time
we drive to South Lancaster
to climb through the loose window
in D's family cottage.

A choice between clean sheets
or car vinyl against our skin.

Rob Sun Ins his hair
plucks his eyebrows, tucks
in his billowy-sleeved shirts
so we know
he's on our team
almost as fast
as he clocks us.

As soon as I move to Toronto
I come out to the rest of my friends
that D and I have been lovers
for two years

and still

the first time
I stand outside a gay bar

I can't help but think
this is a terrible error
I can't undo.

Rob invites the now-
infamous Shawn Syms
as tour guide for our virgin
gay bar experience.

> Shawn
> who three years later
> will also lead me
> behind the 519
> Community Centre
>
> to visit the AIDS memorial
> I've never seen
>
> where he touches a finger
>
> to each name
> of his close friends
> without needing
> to search for them.

Outside Komrads, I ask Shawn,
*What will it be like?*

*A bar*, he says. *It's a bar.*
*With gay people.*

Inside, I turn up my nose
at the suspended
TV pornos
                    with shaved torsos
and cut dicks.

The next day, in my journal,
I'll write:
                *I don't know what*
                *I expected. I just assumed*
                *there'd be a lot more*
                *touching.*

                *I'm glad there wasn't*
                *cuz "normal" bars don't.* [sic]

                *We all had a good time*
                *until Shawn took us to The Barn—*
                *a major hellhole*
                *for pre-ejaculatory*
                *rendezvous.*

Not every gay bar
is just a bar
with people.

The Barn has glory holes
between toilet stalls
and a man
in a Davy Crockett hat
with tail,
glistening
                    shirtless
on the dance floor.

Every fag alive in the '90s
Church-Wellesley Village
watched this guy twirling
in that outfit
at that club
every night.

He defines an era.

When we find Komrads
nearly empty, we bar-hop
to another club nearby
with its sunken floor

twenty or so men
on the periphery
looking down on it.

Nobody dancing.

I can't wait
more than three songs
before I scoff, *Fuck it*.

I haven't come
all this way
to stand around.

First time in a gay club
Deee-Lite loving
my body
spilling across the floor
in all my pearls

I become liquid
rubber
        Gumby
        of the gay bar

        what D calls
        my epic dance moves

        spasmatic elf meets
        *Solid Gold* dancer

so much permission to move
and occupy space, to be a body
without need
to reduce myself

my every gestured
tilt of the rhythm
de-lovely.

# Gordon

divides the world
in two, right? In the summer
of 1992, either you think
the Barenaked Ladies
are shit
or *the* shit

or so it seems to us in Toronto
when they come out
with their hit single
"If I Had $1000000."

I am also out
and single that summer

D and I
release each other

for the first time

between second-
and third-year university.

Finding lovers
in the before times, before apps
mostly means picking up
via bar culture. To find the gays
you have to physically
go to a club.

Stats say we comprise ten per cent
of the population, but
in my classrooms, I'm it.

            Other gays find safety
by identifying as bisexual
and bisexuals find safety
by staying quiet.

You can't walk down the street
homosexual
without slyly checking out
who in the crowd
would choke you to death

in case you don't yet know
what it's like to be trans
today.

Or a woman.

A black kid
in a hoodie.

About this same time
friends bring D and me to the 519
Community Centre basement
for Queer Nation meetings.

We plan kiss-ins and die-ins
protesting our second-class status
and the deliberate
lack of AIDS funding

    it's more convenient
    to let us all die
    than help

though we also in-fight
over respectability politics
sex phobia, white privilege,
and assimilation.

By '92, HIV has become
a right-wing cleanse

governments
refusing medication
international cooperation
or research funding.

Like every gay man
I imagine my future
alone
in a hospital room
nurses will refuse
to enter

until lesbians
on the wards
step in
to help.

AIDS
can't help
but feel inevitable
inevitable
inevitable
inevitable
inevitable
inevitable
inevitable
inevitable
inevitable
inevitable
inevitable

scratch that

needle skipping
through the obituaries.

The religious right preaches
we've earned this horror
which gets a lot more airplay
than science.

I sometimes sit in my dorm room
debating
if it's actually possible the world
will get so paranoid

they'll ship me off
to an island
of homosexuals
as proposed in the US Congress

casually discussed
on the news
                                        and what
am I prepared to do
if it comes to that?

A gay
liberation army
to bomb straight people?

If this sounds like hysteria
you're probably only watching
white people deliver the news.

Read the headlines
for how quickly we destroy
what gets in the way
of capital
                    to understand why the gays
learn to increase their value
by convincing the corporate elite
we have spending power.

Our strategic shift from target
to target audience.

Even in our own
queer camps, health resources
are so limited that when I go
to the STD clinic on Church Street

where one guy
with purple
Kaposi's sarcoma
daubing his face
avoids eye contact

for a genital condition
I think must be HIV-related

because genocide

I'm scolded by the doctor
for wasting his time.
This clinic
is for sexual health, and I have
a fungal infection
from the heat
of tight cut-off
jean shorts.

The point being
gay men's sexual health
in the '90s means treating
or preventing AIDS
so a fungal foreskin
doesn't register in the hierarchy
of gay health. Mine is a straight-
clinic problem.

That's a long circuitous list of historical
complaints having nothing to do
with the Barenaked Ladies and I guess
that's my point.

In '92 in Toronto

—homeland
of the Barenaked Ladies
briefly pilloried for being
neither of those things—

everywhere I look
someone in the news
is planning
my death
                    as people party
to these guys
who make a name for themselves
singing gags
about what a million dollars
of '90s capitalism
can buy them.

Not AIDS drugs.
You can put money on that.

# Rid of Me

PJ Harvey is a slow sell
that first time I hear her
on CD in D's basement apartment
months after our final
agreeable
breakup
                    and the last
weekend she and I will share
a bed in a predictable
grand gesture of good
bye sex.

PJ's sound is so original
and moody, my brain
can't compute
what it's hearing.

I regrettably dis the album
as a perfect example
of the difference
between music
and noise.
                              Spiteful play:
turning D's thrill
into a knife.
                              Sex
with fingernails.
A kiss with teeth.

I sort of intuit
that I'm taking a big step
into a raucous
panic, booming
without D.

I'm facing years of fumbling
condoms,
compulsion, drowning
in alcohol

when I can't remember
how fluids work
beyond swallowing them.

These are my best years
of quiet terror

trying to live
as an adult

drawn inexplicably
to barebacking
drunk
in the park

anything, really
to feel alive
but less.

Feeling incapable
of a man's attention
unless I have one
in hand.

For a long time
everything after D
will feel like a lie
the world is trying
to convince me
is love.

Like Harvey's crooning
off-key "Legs,"
right?
        Ohhh-o-ohhhhh-ho,
        D was gooo-ing
        to be my li-iiiife.

Too-true melodrama
knowing D
has moved out of our condo
for a sex life
we've stopped sharing

as we start again
to make ourselves
family

with distance.

# It's-It

I come to the Sugarcubes late, the spring I move with Matthew and our mutual friend Paul into a walk-up above a plastic surgeon's office, its lobby lined with grisly images of women cut open or healing.

With *It's-It* on repeat, I skip down Bloor Street to Björk's piercing voice, its sonic acupuncture, dopamine at the needle's tip.

Single, this is my year of firsts:

> Doing drag, for one, in *The Unimportance of Being, Ernest*, a little two-hander my buddy Paul and I write and perform at Glendon.
>
> Or that night I walk home alone in drag from the subway as a creepy guy slow-driving down my street tries to talk me into his Mustang. As a man smoking across the road out front of Boots, the cowboy-themed gay bar, yells, *Get in that car! Baby needs a new pair of shoes!*
>
> The driver chases me to the door of the plastic surgeon's office; that must give him a moment of pause. I still regret not getting his plates.

Same apartment where I answer a call from the award-winning author Bonnie Burnard, who complains that I've moved since submitting a manuscript, so she's had to hunt me down via the Toronto phone book and aren't there a lot of Michael Smiths to get through. Thirty-eight.

She wants to publish a story of mine in an anthology that will be my first time in a book.

Where I have my first married man, on a work trip from Chicago; my first threesome, with the first man to admit his HIV-positive status.

Where I bring home from a dance floor broad-shouldered Lee with the loose curls, who gives me the best orgasm of my life, an out-of-body floatgasm, before the cliché cold shoulder.

After ending sex with D—which has been *personal*, sex with a person who wants to have sex with me, in particular—everything else feels awkward. Too much tiptoeing around men's egos and dodging the heavy bricks of homophobia.

Just trying to find another gay can be dangerous since meeting while queer is restricted to geography and puts us at risk of arrest, or being seen, and outed if you aren't already. We have:

(i) the bar
(ii) the park
(iii) the bathhouse
(iv) the sauna
(v) the gym
(vi) the club
(vii) phone lines
(viii) demonstrations
(ix) and, broadly, the city.

We live in sufficient danger to make your blood run. Matthew choked unconscious in a parking lot, two blocks from home, or the drive-by young men sporting baseball bats on any Saturday night. *Faggot. Hey.*

HIV is surrounded by guesswork or rumour, at best, if you can be so lucky, though nobody is supposed to ask.

Resisting stigma also means keeping secrets, like Blake, who turns positive after his first time, or my one lover infected after giving a bj post–oral surgery to a guy who lied about his status, another friend from a broken condom.

These admissions a kind of relief.

Fags build an etiquette, a culture for how to be treated regardless of our status, meaning never discussing status—

(i) don't assume
anyone is negative

(ii) guard the truth
of every
gay man's blood

(iii) all balanced against a desire
to know the circumstances
in which one contracted
an invisible virus we all think
will kill us.

Everywhere, the politics of blood:

Thirteen-year-old Ryan White, AIDS poster child, only guilty of a blood transfusion: A virgin with a viral load finally registers as notable to good Christians.

Our private check-ins with lovers about hangnails or acne or any other potential for transmission.

My activist friends Shawn and Lynn Iding, from *Rites* magazine fame, introduce me to AIDS-related demos:

(i) kiss-in at the Eaton Centre
(ii) blocking Yonge and Dundas
with our pretend-dead bodies.

I can't recall who asks, but the summer of '94 we find ourselves lobbying MPPs prior to the vote for Bill 167, Ontario's Equality Rights Statute Amendment, commonly known as Bob Rae's flip-flop bill, to make same-sex spouses equal under provincial law.

What are they thinking tasking a naive kid—still hammered by the relentless hetero regime of his small town—to lobby homophobic MPPs?

How can they send a wimpy little queer like me to discuss something as important as this?

Perhaps it's my gay-deer-in-the-headlights naïveté they are banking on.

I'm thinking they must be desperate. Maybe I'm the only volunteer they have available for this hater on this day. But I'll admit to being schooled:

(i) if nobody else is willing to talk
you're the expert
(ii) and/or, if you want a job done
you might as well start
till someone more skilled
comes along.

This is how I meet John Cleary, my Cornwall MPP, a white-haired suit with fat fingers and a whisky nose who offers to find my laid-off father a job as a means to refuse to stay on topic;

and the young Mammoliti, a vocal hater, still practicing Ontario politics today, hotter than I expected a ~~politician~~ homophobe to be.

Vote day in Ontario Parliament a few hundred queers gather outside for encouragement before shuffling en masse into the Legislative Chamber, only...the second-floor seating fills quickly, so I get herded into the side gallery

two rows of benches
about thirty padded seats in total

with a few dozen women in prayer-cap buns and men in khakis and short-sleeved dress shirts tucked around me in the cramped space. One of the men shoulder to shoulder beside me.

I've never been in Parliament before, with its dark heavy wood and green carpet.

We sit through final comments wherein one MPP, who has been on the fence, announces he's voting against the bill to honour the will of the majority.

Then the vote is called, results tallied: the bill is defeated 68–59.

The man in the seat next to me shifts his weight.

In the upper gallery, Reverend Brent Hawkes leaps forward in his seat, pointing to the floor of politicians, and hollers, *This is an absolute outrage.*

Everything stops for one long second

like, with the world on pause, we can take it all back.

*Shame on you!* Hawkes bellows. *Shame! Shame!* then the queer upper gallery explodes with his echo.

The world spins, again.

Police gesture bluntly to exit, *C'mon*, so we file out, except, in the lobby and all down the stairwell two hundred queers are backed up, bellowing

*Shame! Shame! Shame! Shame!*

The steps crowded in bodies. Acrid sweat of fear in the air, on my clothes.

Fundamentalists huddle together.
I can't bellow. I can't speak.

We all try not to look in each other's faces. Feeling a fear too great to want to be seen; you do not wish anyone to know you that well.

This is what homophobia desires most of all. Obscurity.

Then I see it, blood on the stairwell railing, blood on the floor.

A chorus sings without me,
*shame shame Shame! Shame!*

Blood on the railing, blood on the floor, first one, then everyone pushing from behind. Falling into each other on the stairs. I see blood on the railing. Then blood on a stair.

Our *Shame!* a wall, a tangible thing, resounding off marble out of the throats of hundreds of us legislated as worth less.

The police finally dump us outside. Queer organizers with bullhorns announce we'll march tomorrow.

Later that evening, in the tenuous safety of my apartment, I ask myself: If I am a person, how can a state think I am less of a person?

The following morning balloons into a day of thousands protesting from Church & Wellesley to Parliament.

I expand, unhinged, unsteady on my legs even twenty-four hours later, like a long slow out-of-bodied stare into a social abyss, bringing me both out of and too much in this moment.

Out of. Too much in.

This moment a kind of inversion of that season in my portable CD player: I'd walk down Bloor to Björk's crystalline voice—somewhere between high staccato and synth warble—coursing electric in my limbs. Like I can't help myself, if I stand still, so I dip and hustle and sidestep and swing revelling in the joy of being a downtown sissy

with Björk's incongruous voice reaching into me at such an authentic pitch I feel her invitation to remake the story of this faggot's body. All I have to do is allow the music to show me how to move.

# Jagged Little Pill

The summer I'm headed to Vancouver
for grad school, I try asking
my ex D
what she thinks of the move
—lez be honest, hoping she'll cry—
but she dances a jig, singing
a ding-dong song
that the wicked witch
is dead.

With a ferocity
unfamiliar to polite Canadians
Alanis's star power rages
viral
across the charts

even more so in Ottawa
with Alanis their homegirl

and Cornwall
riding those coattails.

Having survived
secondary school by being a class clown,
a charmer, the harmless yearbook editor,
that theatre guy with a ponytail, the kid
whose father worked as shop steward
but hung out with the doctor's kid

I'd pined for a future
Toronto, to find more people
like me
                    and, of course,
on my first day of undergrad
at Glendon College, skinny
wide-eyed Michael
had looked around at all my peers
on campus, thinking,
                                        *Oh*
            *these are just the same people*
            *from other*
            *small-town high schools.*

            Soooo,
don't ask me why
I believe a fine arts program
will be fag heaven
                                    but
isn't this ironic: I am the only
gay guy in my MFA
                                        where
one male prof tells me
the first chapter of my novel
about a mill worker who has sex
on the downlow with men in a park
despite having a girlfriend
is a boring subject. Nobody
is interested in a millwright
at work,

though
the only bit at a mill
concerns the millwright's brother
who burned to death
on the job
from an accident with a bucket
of flaming motor oil.
Boring.

In '95, HIV deaths in Canada
peak.
One thousand
seven hundred and sixty-four.

The second
leading cause of death
for young men under forty-four
after suicides.

Um, I wonder
which young men
are killing themselves?
And why?

The good news: 1995
is also the year the AIDS cocktail
begins clinical drug trials
with a jagged little pill called AZT
making every fag's life expectancy
possible.

D too
begins popping pills: estrogen
to accompany her name change

and render my ex-boyfriend
an ex-boy friend.

My first roommate in Vancouver
is a lezzie set decorator
for a TV production company.
Her brother has just died of AIDS,
so he'd missed the cocktail
by months. Irony is its own
bitter pill.
Gail hadn't let
her spare room for the year
her sibling was dying,
but now she feels ready, she says
to bring some gay male energy
into her life again.

She has one rule:
I'm not
to have anonymous sex
in our apartment.

though I mistakenly test this boundary
when I pick up Gary
on a city bus. We talk
and flirt and go back to my place
for a fun night of my tongue
connecting the dots
of his body's freckles.

In the kitchen the next morning, with Gary
in my new bedroom, Gail grills me
on where we met, how long
have I known him.
I think
a conversation on a bus ride sufficient
cuz I'd got his name
but in the light
of day, she and I obviously
have differing opinions
of what "anonymous" means.
Ditto, safe sex.
She doesn't talk to me
for a week. Eventually I'll move out
cuz of her coke habit.

Another male prof that year
tells me he feels he can't comment
on my essay because
he doesn't know anything about
gay stuff
            as if words are illegible
written by a queer hand.

Kinda the same logic
that thinks a straight man's body
is somehow built differently
than a homo's,
                    as if prostates
are the unicorns
of queer butts.

'95 could be my year
to take a cue from Alanis,
grant myself a righteous anger
at people who consider my queerness
untouchable
                unknowable
despite all my writing
beckoning strangers
to know me better.

Rage
is a great motivator
for social change, sure,
if we're talking institutions,
human rights, AIDS drugs,
same-sex marriage, adoption,
surrogacy, health insurance,
permission to be
in the hospice room
with your dying partner, even
if his parents want to refuse you,

rage, sure.
But interpersonally,
anecdotally, I can assure you
nobody
likes an angry faggot.

# The Gossip

Back when *queer* still divides folks
traumatized by the word
from those who want the tattoo

Francisco and his flatmates
in their two-storey
Hastings Street office
converted to a home

host a large party
for the Gossip
    with lead singer
    Beth Ditto
to launch their self-titled EP
in Vancouver.

Or was it *That's Not*
*What I Heard*?
                    It's so long ago,
I don't know who to ask anymore.

The rooftop that evening:
a hidden view of downtown lights, always
a charm for a small-town kid surprised
to be here. The city air at midnight
fresh enough I can smell the salt
of the Burrard Inlet.

A rare night so amazeballs
when I'm in the middle of it
I don't care I'm single
though I hope to change all that
sitting at a merch table
with queer punk friends.

I'm selling copies
of my gay sex zine, *Cruising*,
with photos of my drag personality
Miss Cookie LaWhore, in tennis whites
giving simulated bjs in a park.

                    The internet is a thing,
sure, but Facebook isn't,
so I meet a whack of people
with that rag, especially thanks
to Bryan, who mails my hard copies
to queer bookstores across North
America, just to be nice.
                                        Strangers
from far parts of the US
mail me pics of their butts
long before Grindr
steals my idea.

## Maybe

I should say something here
to embody Ditto and the band
but I'm distracted
by Francisco.

One of the top five men
I'm in love with, the tall
five-o'clock-shadowed Francisco
who seems to have a finger in every
creative pie
will be found dead
in his bed, mid-thirties
with vague enough circumstances
for us to assume suicide
or drug overdose.

> So many queers kill themselves
> it's honestly hard to tell
> if they don't leave a letter.

To say I'm in ~~love~~ lust with him
would be a half story. I've wanted him
to love me, that's for sure, but
the hierarchies of desire
placed me too low
on his dance card
to say anything.

Okay, sure.
Lemme also give the band a try:

Beth Ditto
weaves spells
through the room. Belting lyrics.

Shaking a hand high in the air
for the glory

of queerness, queerness

amplified, a remade verb,
the sound thrills dangerous
and new
a wet joy.

I lean over
to yell with incredulous recognition
in the ear of Bryan beside me

*That's*
*queer* gospel. *She's*
*a fucking queer punk*
gospel *queen.*

Ditto lifts us.

We're all shaking
at the fingertips of that hand, the room
bumping with possibility. Time
made mythic. As long
as Ditto sings, we'll live
forever.
Right, Francisco?

# Survivor

I'll let you in on a small secret.
Better than the year or my age
I can use these albums
to track time
                                    though
this proves tricky with *Survivor*.

Despite being a homo,
I came late
to Destiny's Child

which may tell you something
of my musical tastes and reveals,
possibly, my once-snobby aversion
for anything
considered too mainstream.

Maybe I'm also too damn white.

I tell my husband I know all the songs
on this album but I don't recall
any time I've heard them.

    *Well,* he replies,
    *let's start by listening*
    *over dinner.*

Not five minutes later a dance party
rolls up my legs, through my pelvis
and wiggles down my arms
despite lasagna
going cold on our plates.

I shout,

*The poem writes itself*
*moving through my body!*

*Survivor* opens a current
of kinetic memory

shaking my ass
on turn-of-the-millennium
dance floors.

*Holy, I forgot my limbs*
*used to move like this.*

Then I remember I turned thirty
dancing to *Survivor*
at a club with Kim.
Gorgeous
with the dreamiest eyes
and high Russian Doukhobor
cheekbones

Kim
likes to tease me
how we met at twenty-five
when I interviewed him
for an article I wrote in my MFA
about his work at YouthCO,
a non-profit
run by HIV-positive youth
for youth
but the next time I saw him
I forgot who he was.

We've been overlapping socially
these four years since
but at the end of our twenties
we still aren't tight enough yet
to know we were born
only nine days apart.

We find out on the dance floor:

I'm at the Odyssey
with friends for my birthday.

By happenstance, Kim has invited
a bunch of friends to celebrate
his thirtieth on this spring solstice weekend
that falls between his birthday
and my own.

But only Bryan
shows up to Kim's
big party.

Dancing
to an R&B beat Kim confesses
he's devastated

he'll swear off
big birthday bashes
for the rest of his life

making it sweeter maybe
that I'm having such a good time
I lean in and shout at Kim
over the music to make a pact
to do this every year.

This "Bootylicious"
this "Survivor," this
"Dangerously in Love"
minute is when I decide
to choose Kim
as kin.

I want to fast-forward
three decades
to this past year.

Kim's been working on his archives
trying to outpace terminal cancer.
Multiple myeloma
in the blood.

Reductive
like his shrinking capacity,
what he can eat, how long he has
to nap each day to recover
from simply digesting food

his good hours
trying to outdo the rest.

Ever since that first meeting
Kim's advocated
for queer legacy

to record our lives

since history hasn't been kind
to history that is queer.

Kim gathers queer history.
He remembers facts, trivia,
places, and—his specialty—
people.

And because he has a camera
or knows someone who does
at whichever gig,
every gig, all the time
I'm everywhere
in his archives.
Last time
I visited, he pulled out photos
and videos of our thirties

from the decade to follow
our night of dancing
with Destiny's Child:

walking through the California redwoods,
an afternoon on a yacht once owned
by Judy Garland, road-tripping
the Pacific Coast from LA
to Vancouver, partying
with Pansy Division

whose guitarist swooped in
and carried away the cute guy
I'd flirted with for an hour—
I still resent both of them.

Kim the door opener
always making things happen.
And then keeping track too,
like genealogists who research
their family trees: making time,
keeping time.
                        Saving time.

That first evening
interviewing him, alone
on the YouthCO couch

I think Kim so handsome
I have trouble concentrating
like never before, so I try
taking notes by focusing
just on the page in my lap
when all I want to do is kiss
those pillowy lips.

Kim is so gorgeous
I want his spectacular blue-
green eyes on me

and then
when they are
it's too much.

Kim
vibrates with presence, meaning
when you sit beside him
for the first time
you vibrate right along
with him.

Later that year
I'm volunteering at the Cinematheque
for Vancouver's Queer Film Festival
when some Adonis with green hair
says hi to me
by name.

My first thought is
*I don't know*
*this guy. People this gorgeous*
*don't talk to me.*

Then he says, *Michael, it's Kim.*
*From the interview.*

It takes me years
to admit to Kim
why I didn't recognize him
that day

but I think he likes to rib me
about forgetting
so he can hear my cheeky refrain

that he was too pretty
to remember.
                                    *I had*
*to forget you*
*if I wanted to be happy*

I used to say,
teasing, not yet aware
that's only a good line
when you're young.

# Burn Your Rainbow

*Trust your gut*, Billeh says
when I tell him I'm struggling
with this final album.

*Approach the poem*
*like it's a dick.*

                    Good advice
if you consider the degree to which dicks
have always brought me joy.

So let's climax
with a big applause
as we welcome to the stage
everyone's favourite
queercore trio

...

# The Skinjobs:

**Kim**

already famous
since high school
as the front man for Sparkmarker
on electric guitar
and vocals.

**Laura Lee**
on drums & vocals,
who played in Queazy
and New Years Resolution, now
post-noise

in Down the Lees.

Laura with the chin hair
and a voice
that can sing
anything.

**Mimi** on bass
in short tight curls
and electrical tape
XXs
over her breasts

with a little crooked
James Dean smile
to melt you
at the knees

Joining them onstage
is their motley cast
of go-go dancers
desperate
to entertain:

We have **Darlene**
the Ambassador's Wife
a.k.a. Lloyd doing drag
in his forties
who I first met
at a drag party
of radical faeries:

Vibrating with the thrill
of finally hanging out
with so many queens

I jumped at the chance
to check my hair and makeup
with friends in the bathroom,

where Terwilliger Curves
or Luscious asked

did I want to see the Ambassador's
Wife's cock, and I said, *Sure*
anticipating a prop
from her purse

but Darlene
simply shimmied
up the leg of her pantsuit
and plopped out her real dick.

## Zed

who befriends me
outside the Piccadilly Pub
at a concert
neither of us remember

Zed
in her favourite red-
and-black striped T-shirt

asymmetrical

hair already grey
in her twenties
reared by a fierce
single mother
on welfare

Zed
who will eventually be
in a four-parent family
raising her kids
gender open
until they are old enough
to choose
their pronouns

**Trish**
a first-wave
riotgrrrl
with her zine
*The Makeout Club*

who says she organized
all-ages punk shows across
the Lower Mainland

when she and Kim
were still teenagers

so she'd have a reason
to hang out with him.

and
meeeee
doing **Cookie**

most often wearing
green pigtails, with pink
crop tops and micro-minis
on my furry body.

Bubble gum
punk.

*Burn Your Rainbow*
springs from Kim's seed

when he sends a call
through his network to build
the Queer Punk Collective.

He wants queerdos
to organize
cuz none
of the local press
will cover queer shows—

you can't even get a gig
in event listings, so how
can we find out
what's happening

[
in the time before social media
made posters obsolete ]

As teens, we'd thought we needed
    a city
only to discover too late
    the city
isn't run by queers, nor are
    the police
queer-run, nor the majority of all forms
    of media.
Even queer papers feel pinched
    by advertisers.
This is the story everywhere in 2003:
    the news
reports three million AIDS-related deaths as
    Canadian courts
uphold the AZT patent hoarded by
    Glaxo Wellcome.
Five million people are infected globally.
    Capitalism
better for us all than accessible meds.

Don't get me started on Vancouver at the turn of the century when sociopaths at Canada Customs censor our local queer bookstore under the guise of morality.

It's almost quaint how they ban or steal books and magazines headed for Little Sisters for decades given how the internet has since given us two girls and a cup at our fingertips. But magazines with naked gay people

wow

what a smear

on our social fabric.

HIV-positive, Kim
can't be out
publically
or he risks not being able to travel
to the US for gigs
so he's living the politics.

He sits cross-legged
on the floor
of the Or Gallery.

He's gathered
a dozen of us
to create a listserv
to share event info.

We pool resources
throw a QP Collective
art festival, everyone
organizing whatever
they are into
but we promote it
collectively
among our networks.

Billeh and I spawn
Skank: a literary
smut cabaret

we program
for years
at the Dufferin, a hotel
with a trio of gay bars

one karaoke, one
a dance club, and
the favourite
he smooth-talks us into

a lower bar
with male dancers
every half hour

amateurs
paid $5 a song.

Cabaret begs for a drag queen
host so I try Cookie onstage for
the first time

which feels like plugging
a motherfucking circuit
into the divine.

Meaning Kim
handed my drag
the microphone.

My favourite Skank joke
comes while playing a bit
where I improv asking
the audience if anyone has
questions for Cookie.

Burcu shouts, *Miss Cookie*
*do you ever want to get married?*

And I answer, *Burcu,*

*the only ring I want*

*around my finger*

*is a hairy one.*

From the forehead
of Kim's QP Collective

the Skinjobs also spring.

For their first gig
the look is *Blade Runner*
so I mould a wig into
a Sean Young
look-alike

to sell 50/50 tickets.

The night of the show

I'm heartsick to see
go-go dancers onstage

cuz I would have loved
to have been a dancer.

At intermission, I tell Kim
maybe I'd like to dance

at their next gig, and he says,
*Why not dance tonight?*

Fucking right I do.

Up to this point
I've spent nearly all my life

looking over my shoulder
afraid to be noticed

while dying
to do fun things

that involve being seen.

So let me be clear
that I fucking looove
to strip naked

rub my furry ass
in the front row
of everyone's face

at these rare events
where I'm too busy givin'er
to hate my body.

Each show
the entire band paints
black stripes
across our eyes

homage to
Daryl Hannah

looking to look hot
and fuck shit up.

Often our bandmates
declare themselves
backdrop

to us dancers

encouraged to steal
the show.

We try everything:

blowing
bubbles

stripping

swapping spit
or sweat
with the crowd

deep-throating

bananas

to be explicit

about patriarchy

We rock festivals

with the Gossip, Pansy Division,
USAsexual, Tribe 8, Mirah,
V For Vendetta, the Haggard,
Nomy Lamm

and Tracy + the Plastics—

my new crush cuz
Tracy's two bandmates
are video recordings
of this same performer
in two different wigs

like *I Dream of Jeannie*
as triplets
in an electro-pop band

At Bent, in Seattle, we breathe in
the leather and patchouli

on a dyke dance floor
so many Dandy-meets-Greaser

buzzed-at-the-side pompadours
banging to the Butchies.

At HomoAGoGo,
Cookie introduces the keynote

Kate Bornstein
who later

uses my name as an example
in her talk, as I sob

alone in the upper gallery
cuz my drag name

on the lips of our trans icon
makes me feel not worthy

but more possible.

HomoAGoGo

hits like
*holy shit*

holy shit I'm surrounded
by queers    radical queers

telling stories
in our likeness, building
spaces in our likeness, fucking
*in*
our likeness

everything possible

playing live
in the smell of sweat
between all these
fuck-the-normcore
bodies

Before our last song
at HomoAGoGo

the Skinjobs
invite the audience
to jump the stage

the whole crowd
queer-recruited

as go-go dancers.

You can see us all
here
on the cover
of *Burn Your Rainbow*

a photo collage
Kim made
with images
from that show:

topless, top left
Mimi
screaming
into a mic

here's tsing-ka-ching
Laura
    at her drum kit
bottom right

and Kim
    too pretty
    to remember
he's that shaggy-haired
bottom
left

And you recall the tall
five-o'clock-shadowed Francisco
there
    the middle of the spread
        he's squinting
        biting
        his lip
        giving it hard

that
flawless blonde,
movie-screen teeth,
soon-to-be
Francisco's gf,
that's Jordan
out as trans not a year

though you can't
see his face, here's Matt
Matt. Oh, Matt. Matt
will be dead a decade later
in a freak accident.

I'm back here
in short pigtails
and my
signature look

a creamy
streak of skin
down the centre
of all my hot
pink blush.

None of us came all this way to stand around. Without need
to restrain themselves, hopping onto the stage in all

their pearls, the audience morphs with us into one mass
of liquid rubber. Elbows everywhere, hips cocked, we open

a current of kinetic memory at the edge of our bodies.
The joy of feeling new, a queer finger on the trigger

of a remade verb. We trade dance moves, eager to be loose
with the world. A testament to how living as a queer changes

our relationship to things, convincing us to dip and hustle and swing
to the virus of *this* moment, where all we have to do

is allow the music to show us how to move. A trick
to keep ourselves alive, rocking
                                        the music in our bodies.

## (hidden track: 29/09/24)

can a song be enough
to hold all the truths
we can't bear
without it?

Kim Kinakin is alive
this morning
which will be his last

much like Claire and Sinéad
when I started writing
this book

alive

a record
to replay
an instant

forming a future
dilemma:

I do not want
this printed lyric
to claim Kim
is dying

after he has

imagine I refuse to adjust
my phrasing
that will, this afternoon,
be out of step

that will feel

well

imagine

do I re-record these verses, change
tense
when I speak of Kim

pitch
against silence

erasure

all that dead air

at what point do I say
this, this
is the final cut?

# Liner Notes

Great thanks to the artists included here, for their music, which welcomed joy into my body. Special thanks to those queercore favourites the Skinjobs, who honestly helped save my life: Kim, Laura Lee, Mimi, Trish, Zed, Darlene, David, and all the honorary dancers.

Thanks to UBC Okanagan's Equity & Inclusion Office and the Faculty of Creative and Critical Studies for supporting the first iteration of some of these poems, featured on my vodcast *Soundtrack, a queer oral history project*. Broadcast live, we featured nine queer guests, who wrote their own pieces inspired by some of these same albums.

Our guests were: Ivan Coyote, Suzette Mayr, Zoe Whittall, Lucas Crawford, Ryan G. Hinds, Brianna Ferguson, SJ Sindu, Nicola Harwood, and Hasan Namir. I thank them for sharing their brilliance.

Check out the episodes here:
youtube.com/c/MichaelVSmith71

Thanks to Patrick Grace for selecting "Jagged Little Pill" for the wonderfully queer plenitudemagazine.ca. Thanks to Clare Thiessen from broke press for publishing "Gordon" in a gorgeous chapbook.

Thanks to Billeh Nickerson, my clever friend and *Soundtrack* editor, who made this a better, tighter book. I love you, B.

Thanks to Kathryn Mockler, for all her help, solidarity, and years of friendship.

Thanks to Emily Murphy, Erin Scott, Emma Lind, Norah Bowman, Anita Girvan, John Downes, Tareq Yousef, Thomas Baker, Denise Kenney, Carrie Broughton, Scott Lougheed, Jessica Lougheed, Wayne Broughton, Shelley Pacholok, Trevor Pacholok, Nikhita Obeegadoo, Amanda Poon, Chris Walker, Dana Baitz, and all my friends and family—including my beloved chosen families from the radical faeries and the Inspired Word Café crew—who listened to these poems and offered feedback.

Special thanks to Francis Langevin, who continues to be the best sounding board, idea generator, and karaoke partner this twaddy could wish for.

Thanks to Hazel and Jay and the whole team at Book*hug Press, who are the best kind of people.

And, a final note on D. Writing in present tense about D in the past, but who has since transitioned as a woman, has proven to be a tricky gender conundrum. She and I agreed to use "she" pronouns, regardless of what pronouns she used then, since I'm writing the book now. We've used D, to hold both her names then and now. Thank you for being my first safe place to be queer, D. I love you always.

Jessica Zais

## Artist Bio

Michael V. Smith is a writer, performer, and filmmaker. His poetry has been shortlisted for the ReLit Award, his fiction has been shortlisted for the Journey Prize and Amazon Canada First Novel Award, and his queer memoir *My Body Is Yours* was shortlisted for a Lambda Literary Award. Smith is the winner of a Western Magazine Award, numerous film awards, and the inaugural Dayne Ogilvie Prize from the Writers' Trust of Canada. He is currently a professor in Kelowna, BC, where he lives with his husband on the unceded territory of the Syilx Okanagan people.

# Colophon

Manufactured as the first edition of
*Soundtrack: a lyric memoir*
in the fall of 2025 by Book*hug Press

Edited for the press by Billeh Nickerson
Copy-edited by Laurie Siblock
Proofread by Hazel Millar
Design and typesetting by Gareth Lind, Lind Design
Hand lettering by Michael V. Smith
Cover illustration: Gareth Lind, from photos by janews/Shutterstock and Roberto Sorin/Shutterstock.
Back cover image: istock.com/Blade_kostas
Inside front and back cover image: istock.com/Imagesines
Typeset in Neue Haas Unica

Printed in Canada

bookhugpress.ca